KINGDO
EVOTIONS EMPOWERED ... AITH

# HE
# IS

# KEN
# HEMPHILL

BROADMAN
&HOLMAN
PUBLISHERS

NASHVILLE, TENNESSEE

# KINGDOM PROMISES: **HE IS**

Copyright © 2006 by Ken Hemphill
All rights reserved

ISBN 10: 0-8054-2783-X
ISBN 13: 978-0-8054-2783-7

Broadman & Holman Publishers
Nashville, Tennessee
www.broadmanholman.com

Unless otherwise noted, all Scripture quotations
have been taken from the *Holman Christian Standard
Bible*® Copyright © 1999, 2000, 2002, 2003 by
Holman Bible Publishers.

Other Scriptures used include the New American
Standard Bible (NASB) and the New King James
Version (NKJV).

Dewey Decimal Classification: 242.5
Devotional Literature / Faith

Printed in the United States
2 3 4    09 08 07 06

I dedicate this book to my wife Paula's
sister and her husband:

{ Jimmy and Gretchen Epting }

Jimmy and Gretchen's love for
students has been evident in the growth
of North Greenville University,
where Christ makes the difference!
The rebirth of that school
demonstrates "He Is"
all we need.

# PREFACE

Studying God's Word always brings its own rewards. I have been deeply moved by the study of these simple statements that are scattered throughout the Word of God. It is my prayer that they will minister in your life as they have mine. I thank you for your willingness to buy this book and allow me to be your guide as the Holy Spirit informs your mind and transforms your heart.

As always, I am indebted to my wife, who is my partner in ministry and my encourager in this ministry of writing. She brings the order and solitude to our home that makes it possible for me to reflect and write. She is often the source of ideas that soon appear in my books. Our devotional times together frequently become theological discussions which enrich my understanding.

My children are a constant joy to me, and our growing family provides a rich context for writing. Tina and Brett have been blessed with a daughter, Lois, who is as active as her "papa." Rachael and Trey were blessed with a daughter, Emerson, whose smile lights up a room. It is a joy to watch Katie and Daniel grow in marital love and in the Lord. My family is the context for my entire ministry.

I want to thank Morris Chapman, the visionary leader of the Southern Baptist Convention for calling our denomination to focus on God's Kingdom. He has given me the freedom to write those things God lays on my heart. All of my colleagues at the Executive Committee of the Southern Baptist Convention have encouraged me in this new phase of ministry.

As usual the good folks at Broadman and Holman have been my partners in this ministry. I am challenged by the trust they place in me. Ken Stephens has led Broadman and Holman with integrity of heart. I can't begin to express my gratitude to Lawrence Kimbrough, my partner in this writing adventure. Lawrence is far more than an editor. He is a friend, colleague, and artist. What he does with a rough draft is a thing of beauty.

This book is somewhat of a new genre. It looks like a daily devotional in its format, but it is written to be "bite-sized" theology. I have attempted to explain each of these great Kingdom Promises in its original context and then to apply it to life. Thus, I highly recommend that you read this book with your Bible open, because the focal passages will have the greatest impact on you as you see them in context. You might also want to consider using these verses as a Scripture memory project while you're reading.

I pray God will use His Word to bring encouragement to your heart. And if this book of Kingdom Promises speaks life to you and ministers to your needs, I hope you'll pass it along to someone else.

Ken Hemphill
Nashville, Tennessee
Spring 2006

# FOREWORD

The pulpit area at First Baptist Church in Jacksonville has a beautiful granite piece with names for Christ in gold. They remind us how wonderfully varied and glorious is our Savior.

Dr. Ken Hemphill has uniquely put these names together in a way that will bless and encourage you and also will create greater love for Christ in your heart. Dr. Hemphill is one of our best communicators. He writes in an easy-to-understand, yet spiritually profound manner. You will be blessed as he shares with you his insights about Christ. Dr. Hemphill is also a scholar. His scholarship is very evident as you read through these devotionals.

I am so grateful Dr. Ken Hemphill has given us this beautiful, wonderfully helpful book. Let me encourage you to use it in your personal devotional life. You will be blessed in the process.

Jerry Vines, Former Senior Pastor
First Baptist Church, Jacksonville, Florida

# HE IS
## the Alpha

> Revelation 1:8 "I am the Alpha and the Omega," says the Lord God, "the One who is, who was, and who is coming, the Almighty."

He is the beginning and the end—and the Lord of everything in between! What an incredible statement! But that is precisely what this verse indicates.

When we speak of Jesus being the Alpha or the "first," we are speaking of his pre-existence—the fact that he has always been. *Alpha* is the first letter of the Greek alphabet. *Omega* is the last. By this affirmation, then, John was pointing to Christ's preeminence both in terms of authority and eternity.

Writing also in his Gospel (chapter 8), John recorded an interesting conversation between Jesus and the Jewish leaders. Jesus referred to the fact that their father Abraham had been overjoyed to know that he would witness Jesus' appearance. They responded that Jesus was not even fifty years old. How could he claim to have seen Abraham? Jesus responded, "I assure you:

'Before Abraham was, I am" (John 5:58).

His listeners, shocked at what they were hearing, picked up rocks to stone him for such brazen blasphemy. They knew that Jesus' declaration of his preexistence, as well as his use of the name "I am" in reference to himself, was an affirmation that he was (and is) God, both pre-existent and self-existent, needing nothing else to create him.

Paul wrote about Jesus as the Alpha in Colossians 1:17–18. "He is before all things . . . the beginning, the firstborn from the dead, so that He might come to have first place in everything."

Jesus is timeless. The fullness of God indwells him. Therefore he is the only means of redemption and reconciliation between God and man. Everything rides on this singular affirmation. If Christ is not eternal, he is a created being, and therefore he lacks the quality of God.

But I have good news: he is the Alpha. No matter your present circumstances, he is sovereign God and he will bring his kingdom to victory. Now one question: Is Jesus the Alpha (the first) in your life?

# HE IS
## Our Advocate

> **1 John 2:1** If anyone does
> sin, we have an advocate with
> the Father—Jesus Christ the
> righteous One.

In the last several years we have
witnessed several trials involving well-
known people. As we follow these cases via
the newspaper or television, we are given a
great deal of information about the famous
lawyer hired to defend the person convicted
of the crime. I know if I were accused of a
crime, I would want the best person available to be my advocate.

John declared that we have one. Jesus
is our Advocate.

Having a top-rate advocate, of course,
might cause a client to become cavalier
about sin, to think he could get away with
anything. John addressed this issue without
delay. He indicated that his purpose in
writing his letter was "so that you may
not sin" (v. 1). By indicating we have an
advocate, therefore, John was not suggest-
ing that sin should be seen as a light matter.
Still, we need to know that sin is not

impossible to remedy. When Christians sin, we have an advocate with the Father.

The word translated "advocate" is used by John in his Gospel to refer to the Holy Spirit, who is our "helper" or "counselor" (Jn. 14:16, 26). In 1 John, however, he used it to refer to Jesus, who pleads our case with the Father, who comes alongside us in our time of need as our spokesman.

Yes, our advocate is none other than Jesus Christ, the righteous one. It is the glorified and perfected Christ who pleads our case. He alone is qualified to represent those less righteous than himself before holy God. The entire picture points us to the high priestly role of Jesus, who became our holy and blameless sacrifice and who lives forever to be our advocate before the throne of God, ensuring that our sins do not hinder our constant fellowship with the Father.

This beautiful reality should relieve }us of any anxiety about our salvation. But further, it should keep us from any desire to sin. If he died for us and continues to advocate our case for us, our greatest desire should be to live in holiness.

# HE IS
## the Almighty

> **Revelation 15:3** Great and
> awe-inspiring are Your works,
> Lord God, the Almighty.

We marvel at mighty people —
powerful politicians, bigger-than-life
athletes, wealthy individuals who could
buy and sell most of us many times over.
We have a fascination with strength and
might, whether it be megawatts, money, or
horsepower. But all of the mighty persons
in our pantheon of heroes have weaknesses. Only Christ is the Almighty.

In this chapter from Revelation, John
spoke of the seven last plagues being
poured out on the earth — God's wrath
against sin. The sea of glass is mixed with
fire, symbolizing God's judgment. The
martyrs are standing by (or "on") the sea.
They are singing the song of Moses and the
Lamb — a song of deliverance. They know
that nothing evil can triumph over God's
people, for He is the Almighty.

The word translated "Almighty" is a
composite of two Greek words translated

"all" and "ruler." The Almighty is one without possibility of equal. When those who have "won the victory from the beast" hail Jesus as "Lord God, the Almighty," (v. 2), they are declaring that his power is unlimited. The power of the beast and the false wonders he has worked on the earth cannot compare with the "great and awe-inspiring" works of God.

Notice further in this verse that the thought moves from awe-inspiring power to righteousness and truth. Furthermore, he is "King of the Nations." This not only speaks to his universal sovereignty; it speaks of his heartbeat for the peoples of the world, a consistent theme of the entire Bible—particularly of the book of Revelation. The final victory for the nations has been won by the power of the cross of Christ and heralded by the testimony of his followers.

In the darkest hour of human history, when it seems that the god of this age has won, the conquerors will sing a song of praise to the Almighty. Have you sung the song of the Lamb today? Sing it whatever your circumstances, because the final victory has been won. He is the Almighty!

# HE IS
## the Amen

> **Revelation 3:14** To the angel of the church in Laodicea write: "The Amen, the faithful and true Witness."

Anyone who has attended a church service has heard someone utter the word "amen." Perhaps it was spoken reverently at the end of a heartfelt prayer. In some contexts it may have been shouted boisterously by someone who agreed with a major point of the message. What then does it mean to call Jesus the Amen?

The verse above is in a section of Revelation where the seven churches are being addressed, and the church of the moment is the church in Laodicea. It was located at the junction of the Lycus and Maeander valleys at the convergence of three important roads. It was one of the richest commercial centers in the world, noted for its banking and manufacture of clothing for local black wool.

The church in Laodicea was established by the preaching of Epaphras (Col. 1:7 and 4:12–13). But its spiritual condition had deteriorated to such an extent that it received the severest condemnation of the seven mentioned in Revelation. They are indicted for being "lukewarm" (v. 16), a spiritual condition which had resulted from their great material wealth.

In contrast with the unfaithful people of Laodicea, Jesus is said to be "the Amen, the faithful and true witness." *Amen* is a Hebrew word whose root meaning contains the idea of strength, firmness, and integrity. The idea is that God is faithful, reliable, and trustworthy. He can be trusted to keep his covenant with his people.

Isaiah 65:16 speaks of God in the same manner: "Whoever is blessed in the land will be blessed by the God of truth." The word "Amen" as applied to Christ guarantees the truthfulness of his words, which is further defined by his title as the "faithful and true Witness."

The word "amen" reminds us that Jesus is God's "yes" to all of his promises. How would it change your attitude today knowing that Christ, through his life and character, is your assurance that all of God's promises are true?

# HE IS
## the Author and Finisher

Little things have a way of burning themselves into your memory bank. For example, I loved to go down to our garden with my dad. He was a little old-fashioned, and thus he liked to plow with a mule rather than a tractor. I enjoyed watching the battle of wills as my dad worked with an old mule that was nearly as stubborn as he was.

Once in a while he would let me put my hands on the plow handles and guide the process. After finishing a row, I would look back with frustration to see that my row wandered across the hillside while Dad's seemed perfectly straight. He told me the secret was to focus on a tree or stump on the other side of the field and go straight for it.

In our present context, the author of Hebrews described life as a race to be run, an enduring struggle. And he told us if we want to run successfully, we need more than just the encouragement of a large crowd of witnesses surrounding us. We must keep our eyes on the goal.

Our focal point for the race is not a mere marker in the distance but a person — Jesus. As the "author," he is the source, guide, or pioneer of the successful race. He has already been down this path. Of course, his was not an easy race. He "endured a cross and despised the shame." But as the "finisher," he is the lone example of one who completed the race successfully, the one who has now become our guide and example for life, start to finish. He is now exalted at the right hand of the Father.

And what motivated him to run the race with such focus and victory? He did so for the joy that lay before him, the joy of eternal sonship.

When you find yourself struggling in the journey, when you look back and see that you've plowed a crooked row, focus on Jesus and rejoice in his promises. When we consider eternity, our present challenges become relatively insignificant.

# HE IS
## the Beloved Son

I am blessed to be the father of three wonderful girls. They are now married adults, two with children of their own. But even though they are grown, I love to affirm my girls, and they love to hear it. It doesn't surprise me, then, that on three separate occasions God spoke from heaven affirming his Son, twice with the simple affirmation — "This is My beloved Son."

I think it is important that the first time this occurred, it happened before Jesus had begun any of his earthly ministry. The Father's words must have steeled the Son in his resolve to obey and glorify him.

This statement is drawn from Psalm 2:7 — "You are My Son; today I have become Your Father," as well as Isaiah 42:1 — "This is My Chosen One; I delight in Him." It was not as if Jesus in this moment became something he wasn't. He was eternally God's Son, the Davidic

Messiah, the Suffering Servant who would die for the sins of his people.

In Matthew 17 we are privileged to listen in once again, hearing the Father declare that he delights in his beloved Son. This time the Father gave a command— "Listen to Him!" The command is a present imperative in the Greek, indicating that the disciples should always listen to him. He speaks with the authority of God, for the beloved Son is the Word of God.

The final word of affirmation from the Father takes a little different form, but it makes essentially the same point. Jesus had just predicted his own crucifixion. The Son then cried out to the Father, requesting only that the Father glorify his own name. The word from the Father was succinct but clear—"I have glorified it, and I will glorify it again!" (John 12:28). The beloved Son had lived in such a way that people had seen him and recognized his Father. Now he would die in such a manner that he would glorify the Father.

How wonderful to hear the Father declare, "Well done, good and faithful servant."

# HE IS
## the Bread of Life

> **John 6:35** "I am the bread of life," Jesus told them. "No one who comes to Me will ever be hungry."

As a child, one of my favorite Bible stories was the feeding of the five thousand. I don't know if it was the sheer magnitude of the miracle or the fact that a young lad was given the opportunity to participate in it, but I loved to read that story.

This story actually provides the setting for the first of seven emphatic "I am" statements of Jesus — "I am the bread of life." After feeding the 5,000, he had withdrawn to join his disciples the next day in Capernaum. When the crowd discovered that he had departed, they got into their boats and headed to Capernaum looking for him.

There he confronted them with this truth: they were seeking him only because he had provided a free meal. They tried to avoid his accusation by asking him what kind of sign he would give them to encourage their belief, like when Moses provided their forefathers manna in the wilderness. Wouldn't that make them more likely to believe in him?

Jesus quickly corrected their misunderstanding. The manna had not been provided by Moses. It had come from God the Father; therefore, it was life-giving and abundant. "For the bread of God is the One who comes down from heaven and gives life to the world" (v. 33). There is no room for misunderstanding—Jesus himself is the "bread of life."

This great "I am" statement has clear overtones of divinity and links our life in the closest fashion with Christ. He is the bread who gives and sustains spiritual life. When we feast on him, we are assured of being constantly satisfied. Our only hunger will be for more of him.

My mom had a simple formula for determining whether I was sick or not: my appetite. In much the same way, spiritual hunger is a pretty good sign of one's spiritual well-being. Do you hunger for the Bread of Life? Are you feasting on his Word? Are you seeking his presence in prayer? Expect to be filled.

# HE IS
## the Bright Morning Star

> **Revelation 22:16** I am the Root and the Offspring of David, the Bright Morning Star.

The darkness of night can be terrifying. The smallest sound is magnified. The least movement takes on frightening proportions. But the morning star that proclaims the advent of dawn changes everything. I can still hear my dad's words, "Son, everything will look different in the morning."

John's readers were living in dark days filled with intense persecution. They needed reassurance that a new day was dawning. And they found it in Jesus. He was not only the man who lived and died in Palestine; He is the Messiah—"the Root and the Offspring of David."

We could actually isolate "Root and Offspring of David" as a separate title, but linked with Bright Morning Star it has even greater impact. The first-century readers would have remembered the promise of Isaiah 11:1—"A shoot will grow from the stump of Jesse, and a branch from his roots will bear fruit." But note the subtle yet significant alteration. Jesus declared that he is actually the root from which David grew. He is the very source of the Davidic line! Only one who is eternal can be both root and offspring.

So the Bright Morning Star heralds the dawning of a new day. This reference recalls the prophecy of Balaam. In Numbers 22–24 we find the intriguing story of Balaam, a prophet hired to curse Israel. In his final oracle he declared, "I see him, but not now; I perceive him, but not near. A star will come from Jacob" (Num. 24:17). The Jewish people had long understood this as messianic prophecy.

In our sky, the "morning star" is the planet Venus. In ancient times Venus was seen as a symbol of victory and sovereignty over the nations. Roman generals sought the morning star as a good omen. But where Christ is present, the night is truly passing and a new day is dawning. The Lord of history is the crucified and risen Christ in whom a new day has been heralded and will soon be seen in its full glory.

# HE IS
### the Captain of Our Salvation

> **Hebrews 2:10 (NKJV)** It was fitting for Him . . . to make the captain of their salvation perfect through sufferings.

I had the privilege of being pastor in Norfolk, Virginia, to a large number of our military, and I gained a great appreciation for those whose rank made them leaders. They not only gave orders; they led by pace and example. They blazed the way and represented well those who served under them.

In the book of Hebrews, Jesus is described as the "captain" of our salvation. The word translated "captain" is variously translated as "founder, author, or source." These all point to the same truth: Jesus is the means through which God has made possible our redemption.

Man was created by God for his glory, and yet we have been prevented from attaining that glory by sin. It was therefore "fitting" or "appropriate" for God to provide a way to bring many sons to glory. It was consistent with the character of our loving and merciful God to provide a means of redemption.

We cannot overlook the fact that this required the suffering of his Son. It is in the self-giving of the Son that we see God's heart laid bare. It is "in Christ" that God was at work "reconciling the world to Himself" (2 Cor. 5:19). "He made the One who did not know sin to be sin for us, so that we might become the righteousness of God in Him" (2 Cor. 5:21). How can mortal man ever understand the depth of God's love that led him to give his own Son to atone for our sins?

Yet here it is in its stark reality. The Captain of our salvation was made "perfect through sufferings." This does not suggest that Jesus was morally imperfect prior to his death. (This is explicitly denied in Hebrews 4:15, where he is shown to be "tested in every way as we are, yet without sin.") Rather, his death is described as perfectly completing his life and purpose, enabling him to purchase salvation for us, thus becoming our captain, our pathfinder.

Do you know the Captain of salvation, and are you following his commands?

# HE IS
## the Chief Shepherd

> **1 Peter 5:4** When the chief Shepherd appears, you will receive the unfading crown of glory.

There are perhaps few images of Jesus that evoke more emotion than that of the shepherd. When I was a child attending Sunday school, we received colored cards with pictures of biblical scenes and Scripture verses. I particularly loved the picture of Jesus with a small sheep over his shoulders.

And to prove we don't change much as we grow up—at a shop I've visited in the Holy Land that sells olive wood carvings, the two items most in demand are the nativity set and the Good Shepherd.

In the verse above, Peter was exhorting his fellow church leaders to shepherd those under their leadership freely and joyously. Like a shepherd, they were to lead as examples and not to lord their authority over the sheep. In response the "chief Shepherd" would give them an "unfading crown" upon his return. The adjective translated "unfading" referred to an amaranth, a flower which doesn't wither and revives when moistened with water.

Earlier in this same letter, Peter first introduced the shepherd idea: "For you were like sheep going astray, but you have now returned to the shepherd and guardian of your souls" (1 Pet. 2:25). The writer of Hebrews likewise referred to Jesus as the great "Shepherd of the sheep" (Hebrews 13:20).

One wonders whether these New Testament writers chose this analogy because of the beautiful image of the shepherd in Psalm 23. Yet they likely had something else in mind, for Jesus stood out in contrast to perhaps the greatest threat of all to the early church—false shepherds. "I am the good shepherd," Jesus said by comparison. "The good shepherd lays down his life for the sheep" (John 10:11). "I know My own sheep, and they know Me" (John 10:14).

Therefore he is the model for all other shepherds—not just church leaders but also parents who desire to guide their own children. Look to the Chief Shepherd.

# HE IS
## the Cornerstone

> **Ephesians 2:20** [You are] built on the foundation of the apostles and prophets, with Christ Jesus Himself as the cornerstone.

In this section of Ephesians, Paul was celebrating the fact that Jew and Gentile alike have access through one Spirit to the Father. Thus he declared that they are no longer "foreigners and strangers, but fellow citizens with the saints, and members of God's household, built on the foundation of the apostles and prophets" (v. 19).

Perhaps that last phrase sounds inaccurate to you. You may be thinking of 1 Corinthians 3:11, where Paul stated that Christ *alone* was the foundation. You are correct. Yet there is no contradiction here, just a difference in emphasis. The church stands on a totally unique event—of which Christ is the center—but the apostles and prophets fulfilled a foundational role, bearing witness to Christ and ministering through his church (see Eph. 3:5 and 4:11).

Yet our focus should always be on the cornerstone—the central foundational stone which binds the whole structure together and serves as the stone of testing. It shows whether the building carries out the master architect's specifications. The use of "cornerstone" in reference to Christ not only denotes his position of honor; it also implies that each successive stone must be fitted into him if it is to discover its place and usefulness in the building.

This imagery of "cornerstone" has great Old Testament lineage. The psalmist declared: "The stone that the builders rejected has become the cornerstone" (118:22). The prophet Isaiah wrote: "Look, I have laid a stone in Zion, a tested stone, a precious cornerstone, a sure foundation; the one who believes will be unshakeable" (28:16). The apostle Peter used this imagery to speak of the crucified and resurrected Lord when called before the rulers of the Jews (Acts 4:11). Is it any wonder that he would use the cornerstone imagery on three occasions in his letter?

When you believe in Christ, you can "never be put to shame" (1 Pet. 2:6). When everything around you seems to be unstable, you can build upon the Cornerstone.

# HE IS
## Our Counselor

{ **Isaiah 9:6** He will be named Wonderful Counselor, Mighty God, Eternal Father, Prince of Peace. }

We seem to have plenty of counselors today. We have both the secular and the Christian varieties, the paid and the unpaid, the good and the bad, the invited and the uninvited. It seems like everyone has a solution to our problems . . . even if they can't solve their own! A good counselor will listen, empathize, and point the way to healing, perfectly balancing grace and truth.

And during the dark days in which Isaiah wrote, the people were in great need of one. So he swept back the dark clouds, promising that the gloom of the distressed land would one day be lifted, and that those "walking in darkness" would admit to seeing "a great light."

The cause of this celebration would be the birth of a child. But not just any child! The breadth of what is said of him so far exceeds human boundaries, even the most profound skeptic would have trouble arguing that the prophet had an earthly prince in mind. He must have been looking forward to the day of the Messiah, the Anointed One, the rightful King.

Isaiah saw the child with the royal symbol of government flowing from his shoulders, yet the child was so glorious that one name proved insufficient to describe him. Therefore we find five descriptive titles, including this one: Counselor.

In chapter 11 the prophet identified him as a shoot growing from the stump of Jesse. "The Spirit of the Lord will rest on Him—a Spirit of wisdom and understanding, a Spirit of counsel and strength, a Spirit of knowledge and of the fear of the Lord" (v. 2). This coming one was promised to be the counselor of his people.

Look at Jesus later as he counsels the woman taken in adultery. He offers her grace but confronts her with the truth. Yes, we have a perfect counselor in Jesus. But to benefit from his counseling, we must be willing to listen to him, meditating on his Word, and taking his prescription for our healing: our total obedience.

# HE IS
## Our Creator

> **Colossians 1:16** By Him
> everything was created . . .
> all things have been created
> through Him and for Him.

The Bible begins with the incredible
affirmation that the entire creation—all of
nature and the whole of mankind—are the
love gift of God. They all function for him.
Nothing exists apart from him, and
everything exists for him.

But nowhere do we find a more elo-
quent statement of this truth than in Paul's
great hymn in praise of the cosmic Christ.
In verse 15, Paul declared him to be the
"firstborn over all creation." As the context
makes clear, this in no way suggests that
Christ *is part* of creation. On the contrary,
he stands above and beyond creation.
"Firstborn" denotes both priority in time
and supremacy in rank.

Paul made it crystal clear that Christ is
the firstborn precisely because he made all
things, and therefore everything owes its
very existence to him. Everything came
into being *by* him, *through* him and *for* him.

It came into being *by* (or *in*) him because it occurred in the sphere of his person and power; *through* him, because he was the mediating agent through which it came to be; and *for* him, in the sense that he is the end purpose for which all things exist. The created purpose of everything on earth is to bear witness to him and thus to contribute to his glory.

Also, don't miss the emphasis on the totality of Christ's creative activity— *everything* and *all things*. Paul further clarified this by listing Christ's creation of things "in heaven and on earth, the visible and the invisible, whether thrones or dominions or rulers or authorities." It is possible that this list includes a supposed hierarchy of spiritual beings that some of the false teachers of Paul's day found fascinating. But whatever spiritual beings exist, Christ is both before them and over them.

Of course, there are people still today who are fascinated by spiritual powers and beings, who chase after the new age rage. But why would anyone find such inferior spiritual powers intriguing when they can know and worship the Creator of all things?

# HE IS
## Our Deliverer

{
**Romans 11:26 (NASB)**
The Deliverer will come from
Zion; He will remove ungodli-
ness from Jacob.
}

Because of my many preaching engage-
ments, I have the privilege of worshiping in
a variety of churches with different worship
traditions. I have learned to experience
God's presence in these various musical
contexts. Yet while I enjoy the freedom of
much of the contemporary praise songs,
I sometimes miss the depth of teaching in
many of the great hymns of the faith.

An eighteenth century hymn, "Guide
Me, O Thou Great Jehovah" by William
Williams, speaks with great passion about
the Lord as our deliverer: "Open now the
crystal fountain, / Whence the healing
stream doth flow, / Let the fire and cloudy
pillar / Lead me all my journey through; /
Strong Deliverer, be Thou still my strength
and shield."

Paul, speaking about the unfolding of
God's plan of salvation in history, looked to
the day when all Israel would be saved.

The phrase "all Israel" does not mean every Jew without exception; rather, it refers to Israel as a whole. In this immediate context Paul was concerned about the restoration of Israel to gospel favor and blessing as they turn from unbelief to repentance and faith in Christ.

The imagery behind the word "Deliverer" or "Liberator" is a powerful one. The picture that comes to mind is that of a commanding officer who has just liberated a people held captive. We have all seen such images on television at the end of a long and costly battle.

Our Deliverer set us free from godlessness by taking away our sin. The Bible is clear about man's condition—he is enslaved to sin and thus held captive to death. But Christ is our Deliverer, ready to free us from the restraints of sin, to provide liberty and release from the power of sin and the penalty of death.

Have you met the Deliverer? He stands ready to take away your sins. If you already have a personal knowledge of him, does your life and demeanor give testimony that you have been delivered from sin?

# HE IS
### the Door

> **John 10:9** I am the door. If anyone enters by Me, he will be saved and will come in and go out and find pasture.

When I was a child, there was a popular game show that hid prizes behind three doors. The participants had to choose one of the three to unveil their prize. There was always a bit of mystery and anxiety as the prize behind the door was revealed. Sometimes the participant selected the door with the booby prize. But when Jesus declared that he is "the door," he made it clear what we would find.

If you read this passage in its entire context (vv. 7–18), you will see that Jesus repeated the declaration that he is "the door" in verses 7 and 9. In the first instance, he pointed to himself as the singular, authentic point of entry, that all who came before him were thieves and robbers. This is a clear reference to false teachers whose only desire was (and is) the destruction of the sheep.

In contrast, Jesus promised that those

who enter through him will be saved. He alone is the agent of wholeness and eternal life. His very purpose in coming to earth was that those who enter through him might "have life and have it in abundance" (v. 10).

It is possible that the image of the door is also tied to the reference of him as one who "lays down his life for his sheep" (v. 11). The ancient shepherd would gather his sheep into the fold and lay his own body over the entrance, preventing any of the sheep from leaving and also keeping any wild animals out. Jesus is the door of entrance at the cost of his life.

Yet the door has at least two other functions. First, it emphasizes security and safe haven for those within the sheepfold. And secondly, the reference to the sheep who "come in and go out and find pasture" indicates that Jesus provides for all the needs of the sheep. They have free, secure movement and rich pasture as they go in and out through him.

I'm glad that when I entered in through "the door," I wasn't holding my breath to see what was behind it. I found eternal life in him.

# HE IS
## the Everlasting Father

> **Isaiah 9:6** For a child will be born for us, a son will be given to us. . . . He will be named . . . Eternal Father.

The term "Father" has great meaning to me. My father was my pastor, my friend, my confidant, my counselor. Yes, I was a "preacher's kid," but I never had even the slightest desire to live in rebellion from the principles my dad taught me. In truth, I wanted to embody his godly teaching because I saw the integrity of his life and I knew of his passionate love for me.

The early disciples must have been shell-shocked when Jesus taught them to address the sovereign God of the universe with the intimate term "Father," translated from the Aramaic abba. This word was certainly one of endearment and intimacy that transcended their expectations. Paul wrote in Romans 8:15, "For you did not receive a spirit of slavery to fall back into fear, but you received the Spirit of adoption, by whom we cry out, 'Abba, Father!'" Through Christ he had become a son—

a spiritual reality that seemed to never stop astonishing Paul all the days of his life.

We have already looked at Isaiah 9:6 in our consideration of Christ as our Counselor. We will have occasion to look at it on three other occasions later in this book, but here our focus is on Jesus as the "Eternal" or "Everlasting Father"—the Father of all eternity."

The mention of "eternity" indicates a timeless quality. It indicates that his kingdom has no end. Only one who possesses eternity in his own being can give everlasting life, and this is the nature of the God we serve. Yet it not only speaks of eternity; it speaks of intimacy. This great King of ours cares for his children like a loving father. As the eternal or everlasting Father, he is always present and ever caring.

In Matthew 7:11 Jesus spoke to this intimate care. If an earthly Father knows how to give good gifts to his children, how much more does God desire to give good things to his? I confess that I miss my earthly dad, but I rejoice that in Christ I have an everlasting Father who always cares for me.

# HE IS
## the Faithful Witness

**Revelation 1:4–5** Grace and peace to you . . . from Jesus Christ, the faithful witness, the firstborn from the dead.

We have all seen enough courtroom dramas to know that an entire case can turn on the integrity and reliability of a witness. If one of the lawyers can catch a witness in an untruth or a half-truth, the entire case can fall like a house of cards.

John began the book of Revelation by calling Jesus as a "faithful witness." Christ's purpose, in fact, had always been to obey his Father and make his name known. Think for a moment about the great prayer that stands at the end of his earthly ministry: "I have glorified You on the earth by completing the work You gave Me to do" (John 17:4). He further indicated, "I have revealed Your name to the men You gave Me from the world" (17:6). In his life and through his death, Jesus was indeed a "faithful witness."

In addition—by virtue of his resurrection—he became the "firstborn of the dead." We will return to this great title of Jesus in the next reading, but his resurrection also proved him to be a faithful witness to the Father, "established as the powerful Son of God by the resurrection from the dead" (Rom. 1:4).

His coming, too, while revealing him as the ruler over all earthly kings when he establishes his people "as a kingdom, priests to His God and Father" (Rev. 1:6), will also show him to be a faithful witness of God's eternal reality. John must have had in mind the promise recorded in Psalm 89:27 — "I will also make him My firstborn, greatest of the kings of the earth."

This must have seemed an incredible statement to John's first readers. By all appearances Rome ruled without rival. But the "faithful witness" assured them that beyond the chaos of what appeared, the Son was seated at the right hand of the Father, ruling over all rulers, now and forevermore. Though they were facing the supreme trial of their faith, they could be assured that they had a "faithful witness" — one who was unerring, unimpeachable, and unchanging. So can we.

# HE IS
## the First and the Last

> **Revelation 1:17–18** I am the First and the Last, and the Living One. I was dead, but look—I am alive forever and ever.

Our mind cannot comprehend something being both first and last. But such is the character of our wonderful Savior. He is "the First and the Last."

This phrase, combined with the phrase "the Living One," is an exposition of the truth contained in our earlier discussion of Christ as "the Alpha and the Omega" (Rev. 1:8). This affirmation majestically declares that Christ stands above all limitations of time. He is eternally "the Living One."

John's use of this title links the affirmation of Isaiah 44:6 with the covenant name Yahweh—meaning "I Am"—that was given at the burning bush. Listen with awe to Isaiah 44:6—"This is what the Lord, the King of Israel and its Redeemer, the Lord of Hosts, says: 'I am the first and I am the last. There is no God but Me.'" God is one and he is God alone. Yet Jesus, too, is fully God.

While the mention of "first" reminds us of his creative activity, the focus on "last" pictures him as the finisher. The eternal "Living One" accomplished the incomprehensible: he died, yet he was not simply raised from the dead—he is alive forever and ever! By virtue of his resurrection, "the keys of death and Hades" were given to him (Rev. 1:19). The "keys" signify his authority over man's ultimate enemy. If you know Christ as Savior, you need not fear death. Death is his defeated foe.

"The First and the Last" is repeated in the final chapter of Revelation: "Look! I am coming quickly, and My reward is with Me to repay each person according to what he has done. I am the Alpha and the Omega, the First and the Last, the Beginning and the End" (22:12–13). Here the emphasis is on Jesus' return and judgment. He says: "Blessed are those who wash their robes, so that they may have the right to the tree of life and may enter the city by the gates" (22:14).

The single issue of life and death is this: how have you responded to the one who is both first and last?

# HE IS
## the First Begotten

> **Colossians 1:18** He is the beginning, the firstborn from the dead, so that He might come to have first place in everything.

We are regularly learning more about the impact of birth order. I am the youngest of three. My other two siblings will argue (perhaps correctly) that our parents spoiled me. My sister was the firstborn; thus she was accorded both privilege and responsibility. But I am sure she would argue that responsibility outweighed privilege in her case. My brother would likely argue, furthermore, that as the middle child he was often overlooked.

Whatever the modern day situation, we do know that in the Jewish home the firstborn had unique responsibility that would not be fully shared by the other children.

The term "firstborn" is rendered in other translations as "first begotten." This unique phrase is used in two different but complementary ways, one referring to Christ's entry into the world through human flesh, the other referring to his resurrection. In the case of the first use, I prefer the translation "first begotten" because it avoids the possible suggestion that Jesus was included among the created world.

In Colossians 1:15, we read that Jesus was the "first begotten over all creation," begotten of the Father before any created thing. The writer to the Hebrews used the word in a similar way, declaring that all the angels should worship him as the "firstborn into the world" (Heb. 1:6). Isn't it tragic that some today revere angels and nature when they should be worshiping the First Begotten?

The second usage of firstborn, however, relates to Jesus' resurrection. In this case, being the "firstborn" obviously points to the fact that Jesus was the first to rise from the dead; therefore, he is the "firstfruits" of the resurrection" (1 Cor. 15:20).

And as the firstborn from the dead, Christ will lead all God's people to resurrection. Here again we see the majesty of the Christ—raised from the dead, taking us to glory to be with him forever.

# HE IS
## the Good Shepherd

> **John 10:11** I am the good shepherd. The good shepherd lays down his life for the sheep.

My wife and I lived in England for three years. Because she has a love for sheep, we enjoyed driving through the English countryside looking for them. Occasionally we were privileged to see a shepherd and his dog bringing the sheep in from pasture. Therefore, this theme of Jesus as the Good Shepherd is endearing to most of us, even if we are an urbanite who has only seen sheep at the petting zoo and has never seen a real shepherd.

The word "good" can certainly not be overlooked as a key part of this title. It not only refers to Jesus as *morally* good but may include the ideas of "beautiful" and "authentic." While the Pharisees claimed to be morally upright, their legalism was repulsive and deadly. Jesus' goodness, however, was attractive and appealing.

Also, when we refer to Jesus as good, it is the same as declaring he is God. A man once called Jesus by the name "Good Teacher," to which Jesus responded; "Why do you call Me good? No one is good but One—God" (Mark 10:18). Jesus is indeed the "*good* shepherd."

It must have been rare for a Palestinian shepherd to actually risk his life for his sheep. When he did, it was most likely by accident. In other words, he would have attempted to save the sheep without losing his own life. Not so with our Shepherd. He chose to lay down his life for the sheep. He was not a martyr but a substitute.

The title Good Shepherd also draws attention to another aspect of the ministry of Jesus: "I know My own sheep, and they know Me" (v. 14). This does not speak of a superficial knowledge but an intimate relationship. Jesus compared his knowing of his sheep with the knowing that exists between him and his Father.

The Good Shepherd then made a profound statement about His sheep: "My sheep hear My voice, I know them, and they follow Me" (John 10:27). Do you know his voice and follow him? Then you have eternal life and absolute security.

# HE IS
## the Great High Priest

> **Hebrews 4:14** We have a great high priest who has passed through the heavens— Jesus the Son of God.

Would it help you to know that you have a high priest who can sympathize with your weakness and who desires to plead your case before the Father? Such a truth should give you boldness to approach the throne of grace right now.

The writer to the Hebrews had already referred to Jesus as a "merciful and faithful high priest" in Hebrews 2:17. In Hebrews 4:14, however, the use of the word "great" in relation to Jesus' high priesthood characterizes his supreme dignity. He is seen as being different from and greater than any Levitical high priest.

An earthly priest was allowed to pass through the veil of the temple, but Jesus has passed through the heavens, receiving access to the very throne of God. "The One who descended is the same as the One who ascended far above all the heavens that He might fill all things" (Eph. 4:10).

The linking of Jesus with the phrase "Son of God" may be intended to suggest the two natures of our high priest. Because he is fully human, we can be assured that he can understand and relate to what we're going through. "For we do not have a high priest who is unable to sympathize with our weaknesses, but One who has been tested in every way as we are, yet without sin" (v. 15). Yes, he can sympathize with us in our testing, but he can also give us real help because he is God, because he is genuinely without sin.

Once we understand the greatness of our High Priest, it gives us strength to hold fast to our confession. Do you sometimes feel like you can't hold on in your own strength? That is precisely why we must go to the throne of grace. "Let us approach the throne of grace with boldness, so that we may receive mercy and find grace to help us at the proper time" (v. 16).

Right now is the proper time! You can approach the throne of God with assurance through prayer, knowing that you will be greeted with mercy and sufficient grace.

# HE IS
## the Head of the Church

> **Colossians 1:18** He is also the head of the body, the church.

I was once preaching at a rural meeting in North Carolina, where a number of people from various local churches had come together. After the meeting was over, an elderly man approached to tell me that he had known my father when he was alive. He then remarked that I had both my dad's voice and his passion for the local church. I don't know about the voice, but I do have a love for the church. And why not? It is the body of Christ!

Colossians 1:15–20 is one of the most magnificent passages ever penned about the centrality and supremacy of Christ. Paul spoke of Christ as the "image of the invisible God" and the "firstborn over all creation." But while creation declares the glory of God, there is nothing on earth that reveals Christ like his church. It stands as the zenith of God's creative and revelatory activity.

In Matthew 16 we are told that Jesus established the church, declaring it to be the primary means by which God advances his kingdom on planet Earth. He told us that the church is triumphant, that not even the gates of death can stand against it. He died to redeem it, he was raised to empower it, he sent his Spirit to infill it, and he will present it to himself as his bride. Christ purifies, preserves, and empowers his church. He is supreme over it.

In Ephesians, the companion letter to Colossians, Paul looked at the resurrection and exaltation of Christ in terms of the church. "He put everything under His feet and appointed Him as head over everything for the church, which is His body, the fullness of the One who fills all things in every way" (Eph. 1:22–23). Now that Christ is at the right hand of the Father, the church is empowered to express God's fullness in the world today as Christ did during his incarnation.

Anyone who loves Christ will love his church. The kingdom person will of necessity be intimately involved in the life of a local church.

# HE IS
## the Holy Child

The dean of our school of music at Southwestern Seminary, Benjamin Harlan, looked for every possible opportunity to sing "Holy, Holy, Holy." I can't blame him. If you review the words of that great hymn, you will grasp the significance of calling Jesus the "holy child" or "holy servant."

Luke, the author of Acts, said even the demons recognized the holiness of God's Son. He reported how a man with a demonic spirit once cried out to Jesus in a loud voice: "I know who You are—the Holy One of God!" (Luke 4:34). Isaiah the prophet repeated the phrase "Holy One of Israel" twenty-five times in his book. It was the prophet's favorite designation of God in his covenant relationship with Israel.

This reference to Jesus as the "holy child" clearly has messianic overtones. The phrase "whom You anointed" refers to God's setting apart Jesus as Messiah, a likely reference to Jesus' baptism, when the Father declared, "You are My beloved Son. I take delight in You" (Luke 3:22).

The context is most significant. Peter and John had just been released by the Sanhedrin, the Jewish high court, and had rejoined their friends. This caused the disciples to break forth in praise, quoting from Psalm 2 about the raging of the Gentiles, the people who imagine vain things, the rulers who set themselves against the Lord and his Anointed.

They understood that the words of this Psalm had been fulfilled. The "Gentiles" were the Romans who sentenced Jesus to death. The "peoples" were his Jewish enemies. "Kings" were represented by Herod Antipas, who attempted to kill Jesus at birth. "Rulers" were represented by Pontius Pilate, who surrendered Christ to a mob.

The disciples saw that all these forces could not thwart God's eternal plan for his "holy child." Psalm 2 was being fulfilled before their eyes. The long view of history gave them boldness. Does it give you confidence to know that God is in control?

# HE IS
## the I Am

> **John 8:58** Jesus said to them,
> "I assure you: Before Abraham
> was, I am."

In elementary English we were taught
that proper names are always nouns. But
on this occasion, we have to throw out that
lesson. The name translated "I am" is an
emphatic form of the verb "to be." One of
Jesus' names is "I am."

When Jesus said of himself, "I am
the light of the world" (John 8:12), this
prompted an argument. *How could this man
give testimony like this about himself?* Much of
the discussion centered on Jesus' statements about doing his Father's will, which
caused the Jews to affirm the greatness of
their forefather Abraham. But when Jesus
assured them that their father Abraham had
rejoiced when he saw Jesus' day, they were
totally confused. "You aren't 50 years old
yet, and You've seen Abraham?" (v. 57).

Then the bombshell: "Before Abraham
was, I am" (v. 58). Jesus was aware of the
gravity of this statement. This is why he

prepared them for it with a twofold "amen," rendered by the words "I assure you" in our translation. They had encountered "I am" in combinations such as "I am the light of the world." But here the full impact was felt.

This statement identified Jesus with the covenant God of Israel. When God appeared to Moses in a burning bush, Moses demanded to know his name. God declared: "I Am Who I Am. . . . This is My name forever" (Exodus 3:14–15). Isaiah, in contrasting God with the gods of the nations, noted, "Who has performed and done this, calling the generations from the beginning? I, the Lord, am the first, and with the last—I am He" (Isa. 41:4).

Do you understand now why the Jews picked up stones to kill him? They were left with only two options: he was the greatest fraud and blasphemer of all time, or he was and is the incarnate God. Therefore, when we read "I am," we know Jesus was declaring himself to be the promised Messiah, God in flesh. This is Jesus' boldest declaration about himself. Where Jesus is, God is!

# HE IS
## Immanuel

> **Isaiah 7:14** The Lord Himself will give you a sign: The virgin will conceive, have a son, and name him Immanuel.

We have all experienced the power of "presence" when we were afraid. We have caressed the brow of our fevered child and watched as our presence brought a sense of peace. We have been in the hospital waiting room when no one knew exactly what to say, but the physical presence of family and friends was all that was required to bring comfort.

The name "Immanuel" assures us that God is always "with us."

During the time of King Ahaz, the house of David was beset with enemies, and the king was weak in faith. In contrast to the worldly power on which Ahaz had put his hope, the prophet Isaiah spoke about the wondrous birth of a child whose very name signified a redemption only God could bring. The ultimate fulfillment of this promise would not occur for generations, but the promise was one that brought hope.

A few scholars have argued against the translation "virgin" for the Hebrew word *alma*, which means "young woman." But contrary to what some have argued, the use of the words "young woman" (rather than "wife") suggests a birth outside the normal pattern of childbirth. What we sometimes forget is that a young unmarried woman in Isaiah's day would have been expected to be a virgin. Together with other passages from Isaiah that use the term Immanuel and speak of a coming birth, it is clear that the promise of Isaiah 7:14 is preparing the way for a developing messianic theme.

A few years ago when I embarked on a study of several of the Old Testament names of God, I was intrigued to discover that the last of the names, occurring in Ezekiel 48:35, was Jehovah Shammah, which means "The Lord is there." Ezekiel was speaking of the rebuilding of the temple—the earthly reminder of God's presence. The promise of God's presence was not to be accomplished by an earthly temple, however, but by the birth of Jesus. Only our Savior, Jesus, allows us to experience "God with us."

# HE IS
## Jesus

> **Matthew 1:21** She will give birth to a son, and you are to name Him Jesus, because He will save His people from their sins.

"Jesus, Jesus, Jesus, there's just something about that name," the familiar Bill Gaither tune goes. While all the names or titles we have discussed have significant meaning, none have the emotional impact as the simple declaration "Jesus." We shout it in praise and we whisper it in prayer. We weep his name over our loved one's sick bed, and we breathe it when the storm clouds are gathering. It is a name that brings comfort, strength, and joy.

In the verse above, we have been ushered into the prayer closet of Joseph, who has just discovered that Mary, his fiancée is pregnant. And to avoid public disgrace, he has decided to divorce her secretly. Yet the messenger of the Lord tells him not to fear, for the child Mary is bearing has been conceived by the Holy Spirit. Joseph is to take Mary as his wife and name the child Jesus.

Names, especially divinely given names, are full of meaning. "Jesus" is actually the Greek for the common Hebrew name Joshua. Isn't it interesting that God gave his own son a name that would have been as common in his day as John is in ours?

But the significance of his name is anything *but* common. The name means "Yahweh is salvation." *Yahweh* is the great memorial name of God, and *salvation* is a prominent element of Old Testament hope. This pronouncement set the tone for Jesus' ministry. He was surely not going to fit the popular mold of messianic expectation as a national liberator, but he would deal with a much more universal problem—the sin problem that enslaves man and keeps him from fellowship with holy God.

The name Jesus has become precious because those of us who have come to know him as our personal Savior comprehend the cost of our forgiveness. "What can wash away my sin? Nothing but the blood of Jesus!"

I sincerely hope and pray that you can say the same.

# HE IS
### the Just One

The healing of a lame man created
quite a stir in the temple complex, and his
victory dance gathered quite a crowd. With
the man still clutching Peter's robe, the
great apostle seized the moment.

Peter's message was short and to the
point. This feat had not been accomplished
by either his or John's own power or
godliness. Kingdom people recognize their
dependence on God, wanting him alone to
receive glory. Furthermore, the Jews had
handed Jesus over to Roman authorities
for a death sentence, but God's purpose
was to glorify him. The full impact of their
guilt is felt in our focal verse — "You denied
the Holy and Righteous One!"

You may have noticed that there is
actually a twofold title given to Jesus in
this verse, and both terms have their roots
in the Old Testament. "The Holy One" was
actually uttered first by a man with an

unclean spirit—"I know who You are—
The Holy One of God!" (Mark 1:24). The
demons inhabiting the man knew the truth
God's own people refused to accept.

The "Just" or "Righteous One" clearly
alludes to Jesus as the Suffering Servant of
Isaiah's prophecy. This term is used two
more times in the book of Acts—at the
stoning of Stephen (Acts 7:52) and at
Paul's defense before the Jerusalem mob
(Acts 22:14).

The writer of Hebrews also made it
clear why seeing Jesus as the "Righteous
One" is so important: "For this is the kind
of high priest we need: holy, innocent,
undefiled, separated from sinners, and
exalted above the heavens" (Heb. 7:26).
The Holy One was without sin; thus, he
alone can forgive sin.

When we understand the impact of
this great affirmation, we understand why
Peter saw their denial of the Holy One as
so incongruous. They had killed their
"source of life" (Acts 3:15). But before we
point our finger at the first century Jews,
we must be bold enough to ask, "What
have I done with the Just One?"

# HE IS
## the Lamb of God

> **John 1:29** Here is the Lamb of God, who takes away the sin of the world!

John the Baptist accumulated quite a following with his fiery preaching and his message of repentance. Nonetheless, he continually deflected every attempt by the crowd to exalt him. He was only the voice in the wilderness. There was one who was coming, however, whose stature was such that John would be unworthy to untie his sandal strap.

When John saw Jesus approaching, he announced, *Look*! *Behold*! "Here is the Lamb of God"—a title found only in John's Gospel (vv. 29, 36). The same Greek term is used in Acts 8:32, when Philip helped the Ethiopian official understand that the Suffering Servant of Isaiah 53 had come in the person of Christ. The term appears again in 1 Peter 1:19, when he declared that people are not saved by perishable things but through the precious blood of Christ, "a lamb without defect or blemish."

It is likely that the Gospel writer John picked up on this phrase to present Jesus as more than the Passover lamb. The motif of the Passover runs throughout the Gospel of John, binding his message together. In the Old Testament, the blood of the Passover lamb was placed on the doorpost, covering over the sin of the people. Jesus, however, did not merely cover over; he took away. No longer is man's sin covered over in a sacrifice which must be continually repeated, but it has been washed away by the death of the Lamb.

The genitive in the phrase "Lamb of God" can either mean "Lamb *belonging* to God" or "Lamb *provided* by God." Both are true. The sacrifice provided by God belongs to God, in that he sent his own Son as our sin offering. The wages of sin bring death; therefore, all of mankind deserved to die. The only alternative was for one who was without sin to die in our place. Jesus—the Lamb provided by God—has made redemption for the "sin of the world."

There was nothing limited in his atonement. His sacrifice is sufficient for anyone who will turn to him in faith.

# HE IS
## the Life

{ **John 14:6** I am the way, the truth, and the life. No one comes to the Father except through Me. }

One of the most intimate and endearing discourses of John's Gospel is interrupted by a rather abrupt question—"'Lord,' Thomas said, 'we don't know where You're going. How can we know the way?'" (v. 5).

Jesus was celebrating a final Passover with his disciples. And wanting to reassure them in light of his impending death, he told them about a place where he was going, a place where he would prepare a lasting home for them in his Father's house, a place he promised to return from to take them back with him.

It was at this point that Thomas interjected his honest yet somewhat negative appraisal of the situation. He voiced his deep despair and confusion about the riddles of life. You may recall that Thomas had already expressed his willingness to die with Jesus when he agreed to accompany him on his journey to Bethany (Jn. 11:16).

He knew this was a real possibility if his Master continued on his chosen path.

*But why must Jesus leave? Where was he going? And how could his disciples follow him when they didn't know the way?*

Do you wish you had the courage to be as brutally honest as Thomas? Do you desire to know the answers to life's greatest questions? Then don't miss the radical nature of this claim. Jesus is not a mere philosopher or religious leader who suggests that we follow a certain way, some principle that has given meaning to his own life—He is life! Jesus doesn't simply hazard an answer to life's great questions; he provides life in himself. His solution is neither a recipe nor a religion; it is a relationship with him.

The Jews had denied the one whom God had glorified, and in so doing they had "killed the source of life, whom God raised from the dead" (Acts 3:15). Truly, Jesus alone can give life, because he alone is the resurrected one. "I am the resurrection and the life. The one who believes in Me, even if he dies, will live" (Jn. 11:25).

Do you have life?

# HE IS
## the Light of the World

> **John 8:12** I am the light of the world. Anyone who follows Me will never walk in darkness.

When I was a child, my bedroom was on the back of the house. And just outside my window, a weeping willow tree stood backlit by a streetlight. On windy nights my room would fill with what appeared to be demons and dragons as the shadows of willow tree limbs played across my room. When I could take it no longer, I would cry out to my father, who with one flip of a switch would bathe my room in light. The shadows of childhood fear would vanish.

Jesus' declaration that "I am the light of the world" would have instantly and dramatically caught everyone's attention. The setting was the Feast of Tabernacles. A part of that celebration was the much anticipated lighting of the festive golden lamps. These lamps reminded the worshipers of the pillar of fire which God had used to lead Israel during those long-ago years of wilderness wandering.

Perhaps you have already noticed that Jesus never said he would provide *enlightenment*, as other religious leaders claimed. He declared instead that he was the source of all light. It was Yahweh (Jehovah) who spoke light into being, and the connection of the word "light" with the declaration "I am" made this declaration even more stunning. Jesus was the very glory of God. He was and is that pillar of light which gives life.

But this light does not belong to mankind in general. Only those who follow him are delivered from darkness. The word "follows" in verse 12 carries the idea of *continuously* following. We experience the light of his presence only as we are wholeheartedly following him. We don't have to walk in darkness.

One final note: you may recall that Jesus also said that his kingdom followers would be the "light of the world" (Matt. 5:14). Our light is not of the same essence as his, but it is the clear reflection of it. Like the moon reflects the light of the sun, so we are intended to reflect the light of God's Son.

# HE IS
## the Lion of Judah

> **Revelation 5:5** The Lion from the tribe of Judah, the Root of David, has been victorious.

The lion has long been a symbol of strength and victory. From antiquity we find it emblazoned on armor and standards carried into battle. We refer to the lion as the king of the jungle. If you are a C. S. Lewis fan, you fell in love with Aslan the lion that was slain.

In the last book of the Bible, John gave us a glimpse into the heavenlies. He was grieved that "no one in heaven or on the earth or under the earth" was able to break the seven seals and open the scroll (Rev. 5:3). But his wailing was stopped by one of the elders, who comforted him with the news that the Lion of Judah had won the victory and thus was qualified to open the scroll.

The expression "Lion of Judah" occurs only here in the Bible, alluding to the first messianic prophecy in Genesis 49:9–10. Judah is pictured in that passage as a young lion that has returned from victory, about whom it is said, "The scepter will not depart from Judah, or the staff from between his feet, until He whose right it is comes and the obedience of the peoples belongs to Him," until all nations of the earth come under the reign of their rightful King.

Notice too that John identified the Lion of Judah with the "Root of David." This is likely an allusion to the prophecy in Isaiah 11:1 — "A shoot will grow from the stump of Jesse, and a branch from His roots will bear fruit." The royal family of David was pictured as a tree that had fallen, but out of it had sprung the one who would restore the kingly rule.

When John looked for the Lion, he saw "one like a slaughtered lamb" (v. 6). The final victory of Christ is possible only because he willingly suffered as the Lamb of sacrifice.

All these images point to an incredible truth: the Messiah "has been victorious." By his incarnation, death, and resurrection, Christ has triumphed over all the powers of Satan. Are you experiencing his victory?

# HE IS
## the Lord of All

**Acts 10:36** He sent the message . . . proclaiming the good news of peace through Jesus Christ — He is Lord of all.

There are certain events in life that help us to see a fundamental truth in bold relief. Once seen, it becomes forever etched on our hearts and it impacts all we do. Such an event for Peter and for the early church was the conversion of Cornelius.

Cornelius was a centurion of the Italian Regiment. He was a Gentile who feared God, prayed always to him, and did good deeds for the Jewish people. God honored the desire of this devout man who was earnestly seeking him, and instructed him to send for Peter.

As Peter was praying on the housetop, the Lord spoke to him in a vision. He saw a sheet being lowered to the earth filled with animals considered unclean by the Jews. He was instructed to eat but he refused. Yet the voice continued to repeat the instruction three times, saying, "What God has made clean, you must not call common"

(Acts 10:15). While Peter was pondering this vision, the men from Cornelius came for him.

After arriving at the house of Cornelius, Peter began his speech to them with a confession: "In truth, I understand that God doesn't show favoritism" (v. 34). What an insight! This had been a truth the Old Testament Jews had failed to comprehend—that God had chosen them to join him in reaching the nations. Even the early Jews who accepted Jesus as their Messiah had the same parochial view of God.

Thus Peter admitted that his mind was just now taking hold of a truth which should have been clear to him at Pentecost, when the message was declared in every man's tongue. He now understood that the person who fears God in every nation is "acceptable" to him (v. 35). Relationship with God was never intended to be exclusive to the Jews, because he is "Lord of all."

Do you believe that Jesus is Lord of all? Does your giving and your going reflect the desire of the Lord that all may come to know him?

# HE IS
## the Lord of Glory

> **1 Corinthians 2:8** If they had known it, they would not have crucified the Lord of glory.

The Corinthian letter has always been one of my favorites. The church family in Corinth was diverse, to say the least. And sometimes this diversity led to a factious spirit.

There were some in Corinth who were impressed by flowery speech and the rhetoric of wisdom. Thus Paul had determined to focus on preaching Jesus simply, for he knew that those who were "mature" would recognize the wisdom of Christ without all the lofty language (v. 6).

The wisdom that Paul preached was "hidden in a mystery" (v. 7), unable to be discerned by human wisdom. It is a wisdom that must be revealed by the Spirit of God, who searches "the deep things of God" (v. 10). And the sure evidence that none of the rulers of this age understood God's wisdom was their role in the crucifixion of the "Lord of glory."

What divine irony! The very men who attempted to do away with Jesus unwittingly participated in carrying out God's divine purpose determined before the ages. They thought they were killing a messianic pretender, a blasphemer. But if they had understood the enormity of rejecting him, they would not have done so.

The title "Lord of glory" is seen by many to be the most magnificent title given to Christ. James referred to Jesus as our "glorious Lord" (James 2:1). And in John's Gospel we find a similar idea. "We observed His glory, the glory as the One and Only Son from the Father, full of grace and truth" (John 1:14). In the Old Testament, God's glory was manifest on a smoke-shrouded mountain, in the pillar of fire, and in the cloud filling the temple. But once Jesus came, God's glory was manifest in *him*.

The Lord of all ages is thus the Lord of final glory, for himself and for all his people. Paul concluded that if the rulers of this age had understood this, they never would have rejected him. But *we* understand! May we never be guilty of rejecting him through our apathy or unbelief..

# HE IS
## the Man of Sorrows

> Isaiah 53:3 (NASB)  He was
> despised and forsaken of men,
> a man of sorrows and acquainted
> with grief.

"Man of sorrows" has a rather somber feel, doesn't it? Yet I think you may discover that this name will become one of the titles of Jesus that will be most precious to you.

When Isaiah first began to describe him, he saw him as a "young plant," like a shoot that is often cut off before maturity, like a "root out of dry ground" (Isa. 53:2). No one expects much from a plant like that. Jesus' background was such that few could suspect that he was born with royal blood, that he was in the lineage of Jesse and David.

We have so romanticized the story of Jesus' beginnings, we forget that his conception through a virgin left many scandalized. For some he would always be an illegitimate child. Remember the accusation of the Jews: "We weren't born of sexual immorality" (John 8:41). For others he was nothing more than a carpenter's son, a handyman (Matt. 13:55).

Thus Isaiah prophesied, "He was despised and rejected by men." John stated this same truth in its most blunt form: "He came to His own, and His own people did not receive Him" (John 1:11). But the deep sorrow of Jesus came when he took upon himself the sin of the world and received the chastisement that belonged to us.

I can still vividly remember watching *The Passion of the Christ* by Mel Gibson. During the brutal beatings, most viewers had to look away. We could not bear to look upon him. But as we watched the drama unfold, tears of joy welled up in our eyes as we comprehended the truth of his suffering. "He Himself bore our sicknesses, and He carried our pains. . . . He was pierced because of our transgressions, crushed because of our iniquities. . . . The Lord has punished Him for the iniquity of us all" (vv. 4–6).

The Man of Sorrows took our place. He "who did not know sin" bore our sins, "so that we might become the righteousness of God in Him" (2 Cor. 5:21).

# HE IS
## Our Master

{ **Luke 5:5** "Master," Simon replied, "we've worked hard all night long and caught nothing! But at Your word, I'll let down the nets." }

Can you sense Peter's frustration? He may not have been an expert at many things, but he knew fishing. This was his turf, and now a novice fisherman was telling him what to do.

You are probably familiar with the story. Jesus was teaching by the side of Lake Gennesaret when the crowd literally pressed him to the water's edge. Seeing two fishing boats nearby, he commandeered one for his floating platform and continued his message. When the sermon was complete, he instructed Simon, "Put out into deep water and let down your nets for a catch" (v. 4).

Do you identify with the conflict raging in Peter's mind? He and his partners had fished all night with nothing to show for it. They were exhausted and frustrated because there would be no paycheck today. He must have thought,

"This guy may be a great teacher, but I'm the expert here." Yet to Peter's credit, he obeyed the one he called "Master."

The term *master* only occurs on six occasions in the Bible, and all are found in Luke's Gospel. It means "one who is set over," such as a military officer or the commander of a ship.

In fact, these same fishermen later uttered this word again in a slightly different setting. In Luke 8:24, while out on a boat in the middle of a stormy night, they cried out; "Master, Master, we're going to die." They had used all of their considerable knowledge and skill to save themselves. But in a final act of desperation, they woke Jesus, who calmed the storm and rebuked his disciples for their unbelief. "Who can this be?" they asked themselves. "He commands even the winds and the waves, and they obey Him!" (Luke 8:25).

All of these stories have a common theme: Jesus has absolute authority over our lives. Thus, like the fishermen, we must obey when all the circumstances of life and reason dictate against it. There is no realm where he is not qualified as Master.

# HE IS
## Our Mediator

> **1 Timothy 2:5** For there
> is one God and one mediator
> between God and man,
> a man, Christ Jesus.

One of the intriguing personalities of
the Old Testament is Job. You may recall
that he underwent severe testing and yet
remained faithful to the Lord. But he pled
for someone who would mediate between
himself and God. After all, the Lord was
not a man Job could just sit and talk to.
"There is no one to judge between us, to
lay his hand on both of us" (Job 9:33).

But Job's plea has now been answered
in Christ Jesus, who is the one mediator
between God and man.

Notice that this great "He Is" statement
is found in a section where Paul was
encouraging believers to pray for all men.
Have you ever paused to think that the
foundation of all prayer is the mediatory
role of Christ? He is our mediator both in
terms of redemption and intercession.

The essence of kingdom focused
praying is found in verses 3–4: "It pleases

God our Savior, who wants everyone to be saved and to come to the knowledge of the truth." We are required to pray for all persons because there is only one God, who created all peoples and thus desires them to be saved.

Since there is only one God, there can likewise only be one mediator. And only Christ is qualified, because he is fully God and fully man. Through his perfect life and substitutionary death, he met all the demands of God's law and gave himself as a "ransom for all" (v. 6), as the price required to free us from slavery. Don't forget that sin enslaves us all. Therefore, all of us require a mediator who can free us from slavery and rightly relate us to a holy God.

Jesus Christ died for all the people of the earth, and his desire is that all be saved. But how will this good news get to those at the ends of the earth?

Prayer is the foundation for kingdom advance. We must follow Paul's direction that "petitions, prayers, intercessions, and thanksgivings be made for everyone" (v. 1). Our prayers open the doors for those who herald the gospel.

# HE IS
## the Messiah

{ **Luke 2:11** Today a Savior, who is Messiah the Lord, was born for you in the city of David. }

Have you ever heard a story so many times that it begins to lose its impact? As my dad aged, he would often repeat a story about his childhood that I had heard on numerous occasions. Because of my great love for my dad, however, I would listen with rapt attention as if I were hearing the story for the first time.

Now that my dad is gone, I am glad that he repeated those great stories—just as today we are looking at a verse that should grow more precious to us every time we hear it.

The original story of Jesus' birth was heralded by an angel of the Lord to lowly shepherds. Isn't it interesting that a history-altering event like this would be declared to ordinary men busy at a rather mundane task? At the heart of the story is the incredible good news that the long awaited Messiah had been born.

The Greek *christos* translates the Hebrew *messiah*, which means "anointed one." *Anointing* in the Old Testament was reserved for special servants like the priest or king. Yet the Jews looked for a day when God would send a unique Messiah to be the deliverer of his people.

Thus we are told that the Messiah is also Savior, a title used only here in the synoptic gospels. Our Messiah is the one who saves us from sin and alienation, from all dangers . . . ultimately from death.

So hear this story again for the first time. Our Savior is the one anointed by God as prophet, priest, and king. As such, he is Lord—a word often used in the Old Testament to translate the great covenant name Yahweh. Our Messiah is God in the flesh.

As you hear this familiar story, I challenge you to think seriously about a couple of questions. Is the Messiah your personal Savior? Have you turned from your self-rule and asked him to be your Savior and Lord? If not, why not do so right now? If so, do you trust him to provide for your every need?

# HE IS
## the Mighty God

> Isaiah 9:6 He will be named
> Wonderful Counselor, Mighty
> God, Eternal Father, Prince
> of Peace.

"What a mighty God we serve! /
Angels bow before him / Heaven and earth
adore him." So goes a portion of the lyrics
from a song that has had a long run of
popularity. Perhaps its hand-clapping
rhythm is what has made it popular, but
the truth of its words is what is most
important.

We have already looked at two titles
that come from this text—Counselor and
Everlasting Father. We will look at two
others before this book is ended—Prince of
Peace and Wonderful. For now, we focus
on him as Mighty God.

Isaiah wrote to a suffering people
whose life had been one of gloom and
despair. They needed a word of hope. Yet
Isaiah promised that hope was on the way.
He saw the dawn of a new light for the
people walking in darkness, those who had
dwelt in the shadow of death (v. 2). Hope

would come through the birth of a child, whose greatness is such that one name will not suffice.

The title "Mighty God" speaks of his sovereign might and heroic nature. Like the Israelites of old, we should take comfort in knowing that we serve a God whose power is unlimited. There is nothing you will face today that moves beyond the power of Mighty God.

Do you remember the song of praise that Mary sang to God when she visited Elizabeth after learning of the babe in her womb? "Surely, from now on all generations will call me blessed, because the Mighty One has done great things for me" (Luke 1:48–49). She recognized that the miracle in her womb was only possible through the action of sovereign, almighty God.

What do you need to surrender to Mighty God? What keeps you from doing so? Is it your lack of conviction that God has all might? Remember Daniel's conclusion: "The people who know their God will be strong and take action" (Daniel 11:32). Those of us who know him by faith can trust in his power and victory.

# HE IS
## the Only Begotten Son

> **John 3:18 (NASB)** He has
> not believed in the name of the
> only begotten Son of God.

Nicodemus was a good, religious man. One might even call him a seeker. He came to Jesus with a level of belief. But based on Jesus' response to him, he must have been troubled by a single issue: *How can any person enter the kingdom of God?*

It is in this context that we find the favorite verse of many—John 3:16. It contains such profound truths, we stand before it speechless. It speaks of God's infinite and profound love, his universal love, his sacrificial, initiating love. The immensity of the gift is staggering—his one and only Son.

Why was God moved to provide such a unique and priceless gift? Because everything was at stake! God's heartbeat, echoed throughout Scripture, is that all the peoples of the earth would escape judgment and enjoy salvation—"that the world might be saved through Him" (v. 17).

Verse 18, then, puts everything in perspective. The Scripture is clear that God's intention is for all humanity to be saved (Acts 17:30–31 and 1 Tim. 2:4). Yet man, created in God's image, has been given free will which requires a personal response.

John actually repeated some form of the word "believe" three times in verse 18, underlining the enormity of refusing to accept God's Son. The place where we will spend eternity is not based on some uncaring force or irresistible fate; it is based on our response to God's "only begotten Son."

We encountered this phrase for the first time in John 1 — "The Word became flesh and took up residence among us. We observed His glory, the glory as the One and Only Son from the Father, full of grace and truth" (John 1:14). The title "only begotten" assures us that Jesus eternally has the same nature as the Father. Furthermore, it declares his absolute uniqueness in providing the way to the Father. Since Jesus is the "one and only Son," to reject him brings condemnation. God's desire is that all men receive him.

# HE IS
## the Prince of Peace

{ **Isaiah 9:6** He will be named
Wonderful Counselor, Mighty
God, Eternal Father, Prince
of Peace. }

I grew up in an era marked by the
peace symbol, a time when the Vietnam
War polarized the nation. I was in college
when the draft was enacted, and I still
remember the day when I was told that one
of my college friends was killed in that
conflict.

Peace seems even more elusive today
than it was when I graduated from college.
War came to our shores on September 11,
2001, and our new enemy—the terrorists—
are elusive and thus more difficult to
defeat. Will our children and our children's
children ever know peace?

We return once again to the promise of
Isaiah 9:6. All the names mentioned in this
verse find their climax in this great affirmation—"Prince of Peace." Again, these
words were written to a people living in
deep despair and darkness. Yet one was
prohesied who would shatter the burden-

some yoke of their oppressors. No promise of peace could be more vivid than verse 5: "For the trampling boot of battle and the bloodied garments of war will be burned as fuel for the fire."

But his peace is not simply a cessation of strife. It is much, much more! It is a life of personal well-being and hope — of salvation, blessing, happiness, and fullness. Just listen to the implications as spelled out in verse 7: "The dominion will be vast, and its prosperity will never end. He will reign on the throne of David and over his kingdom to establish and sustain it with justice and righteousness from now on and forever. The zeal of the Lord of Hosts will accomplish this."

Ultimately, his peace will envelop all the earth and its peoples. "I will cut off the chariot from Ephraim and the horse from Jerusalem. The bow of war will be removed, and He will proclaim peace to the nations" (Zech. 9:10). Those who know the Prince of Peace will one day join him in extending his reign to the nations. We know the message that will bring peace, and we must declare it to the nations.

# HE IS
## Our Redeemer

> **Job 19:25** But I know my living Redeemer, and He will stand on the dust at last.

Job was placed under severe testing when the circumstances of his life were radically changed. Perhaps the most difficult element of it was the accusation of his friends, who were quick to give their diagnosis of the situation.

In his response to one of them, Job made a great declaration—"I know my living Redeemer"—echoing his conviction that one day he would see God. This one who was his redeemer would also become his vindicator.

The idea of a *redeemer* is a concept which the Jew would clearly understand. For example, Leviticus 25 taught that the land belonged to the Lord and was given in stewardship to man. For this reason, it could not be permanently sold (v. 23). If a man became destitute and had to sell his land, his nearest relative could come and redeem what his brother had sold (v. 25).

Later, the psalmist wrote: "May the words of my mouth and the meditation of my heart be acceptable to You, Lord, my rock and my Redeemer" (Ps. 19:14). The image of the rock indicates refuge, and the word "Redeemer" indicates that God was his champion.

The most beautiful and moving picture of a redeemer in the Old Testament, however, is the story of Hosea and Gomer. Hosea was a prophet who was married to a harlot. One day Hosea saw Gomer being sold on the slave market. But with unprecedented love and grace, he bought his wife's freedom. He became her redeemer.

The story doesn't stop here, though. All the images of a redeemer point to Christ, who "has redeemed us from the curse of the law by becoming a curse for us" (Gal. 3:13). "God sent His Son . . . to redeem those under the law" (Gal. 4:4–5). "He gave Himself for us to redeem us from all lawlessness and to cleanse for Himself a special people, eager to do good works" (Titus 2:14).

Do you know your Redeemer? And are you eager to please him?

# HE IS
## the Resurrection and the Life

> **John 11:25** I am the
> resurrection and the life.
> The one who believes in Me,
> even if he dies, will live.

As a pastor, I accompanied many
families on that difficult trip to the grave-
yard as they buried a family member or
loved one. In recent years I have had to
make that same trip myself—first with my
dad, then my mom.

But I cannot imagine how intense the
pain must be for the individual who has no
hope or assurance of ever seeing their dear
one again. While my grief was profound, it
was tempered by the firm assurance that
Jesus is "the resurrection and the life."

The two sisters of Lazarus struggled
with the death of their brother. Typical
to grief, Martha was looking for someone
to blame, and Jesus was the most likely
candidate. She asserted that if he had been
present, Lazarus would not have died.
And though she properly understood and
believed that he would be resurrected at
the last day, Jesus' reply to her was star-

tling indeed: "I am the resurrection"—
in the present tense.

Martha spoke of resurrection as if it
were only a future gift of God to be dis-
pensed by Christ at the end of time. But
Christ's assertion required that she focus not
on resurrection but on him. He is not the
*dispenser* of resurrection; he *is* resurrection!

Notice that "resurrection" is the first
word Jesus mentioned. But it is taken up
into the larger concept of "life," which is
already ours today in Christ.

We are reminded of Paul's shout of
triumph: "Death has been swallowed up
in victory" (1 Cor. 15:54). This victory is a
present tense reality for those who are in
Christ. It is why Jesus could promise,
"Everyone who lives and believes in Me
will never die—ever" (John 11:26). When
we are hidden in Christ, death has no
authority over us. When we lay down this
earthly body, our life in Christ will become
resurrection life!

There is only one permanent cure for
the fear of death—life! Eternal life! And
this life is only found in our Lord and
Savior, Jesus Christ.

# HE IS
## Our Rock

> **1 Corinthians 10:4** They drank from a spiritual rock that followed them, and that rock was Christ.

The Corinthian church was anything but boring. There were believers who saw themselves as spiritually exalted, which left others feeling spiritually inferior. This led to divisions in the church and distorted understandings of biblical truths.

Some Corinthians, for example, had developed a view of the Lord's Supper which bordered on the magical. If they took the elements on a regular basis, they thought they could live as they pleased. We see a similar disconnect today when people wear a cross as a good luck charm or treat church membership as little more than a fire insurance policy.

Paul warned the Corinthians about such spiritual arrogance by reminding them of the judgment that came upon the Israelites, who had likewise enjoyed God's rich supply of spiritual blessings as they traveled in the wilderness. The linking of "rock" and "spiritual drink" would have brought to mind the stories of the striking of the rock from which water miraculously flowed (Exod. 17 and Num. 20).

Yet Paul quickly focused this analogy on Christ, identifying him with the "rock" image of the Old Testament, thus identifying him as Jehovah.

In the Song of Moses, recorded in Deuteronomy 32, the image of Yahweh as the "Rock" occurs frequently (vv. 4, 15, 18, 30, 31). Listen to verse 4: "The Rock—His work is perfect; all His ways are entirely just." He warned them about scorning or ignoring the Rock. In speaking of other nations, Moses declared: "But their 'rock' is not like our Rock" (v. 31). The psalmist also picked up on this imagery, declaring, "The Lord is my rock, my fortress, and my deliverer" (Ps. 18:2).

There are certainly implications here of the pre-existent Christ and the oneness of God, the source of all the blessings Israel received as they traveled. But the over-whelming truth is that he is our Rock today—our provider, the source of all good things, our rock of refuge, our strength.

# HE IS
## the Rose of Sharon

> **Song of Songs 2:1** I am a rose of Sharon, a lily of the valleys.

My dad loved roses! I can still remember the excitement that any gardening catalog produced in him upon its arrival. Dad would quickly flip to the section containing roses to see if a new variety was being offered. The new rose was quickly ordered and planted, and the entire family waited with rapt eagerness to see it in bloom.

This title "Rose of Sharon" has likewise become precious to many believers, yet it occurs only once in the Bible. The Song of Songs tells of the great love between Solomon and his bride, Shulamith. In the first chapter the couple exchanges expressions of desire, encouragement, and endearment as they ponder their great love for one another. Some of the images seem a bit quaint to us since they come from a rural setting long ago. Nonetheless, it is clear that Solomon greatly admires her stunning beauty.

Shulamith's response to Solomon, which contains the description "rose of Sharon" and "lily of the valleys," may seem boastful, but the very opposite is true. The beloved modestly and humbly compares herself to the common wildflowers of the valley of Sharon.

The word translated "rose" is derived from a Hebrew word meaning "to form bulbs," and thus may be more akin to a crocus, narcissus, or daffodil. The reference to the lily may be used of any one of a number of flowers, ranging from the lotus of the Nile to the wildflowers of Palestine. Thus the bride humbly compares herself to a common wildflower that bursts into bloom in the midst of the everyday brambles of life. She is not locked up in some private garden but is available to all.

Isaiah described the coming Messiah as one who had "no form of splendor that we should look at Him, no appearance that we should desire Him" (Isa. 53:2). Yet like Solomon, when you have fallen in love with Christ, he is like a rose among thorns. Daily he bursts into glorious bloom in the midst of the brambles of your life.

# HE IS
## Our Savior

> **2 Timothy 1:10** This has now been made evident through the appearing of our Savior Christ Jesus.

The announcement that opens the pages of the New Testament brings this hope: "She will give birth to a son, and you are to name Him Jesus, because He will save His people from their sins" (Matt. 1:21). This declaration is made all the more precious because it addresses our greatest need. Our sin has alienated us from a holy God who created us to live in a permanent relationship with him. Thus our greatest need is for a Savior who can deliver us from our sin.

In the above text from 2 Timothy, Paul was encouraging his readers from prison. He spoke of their salvation and calling, purposed by God in Christ Jesus before time began. The idea of God's eternal purpose from eternity past may be beyond our comprehension, but it has now been made evident by the birth of "our Savior Christ Jesus."

To begin with, he has "abolished death" (v. 10). *Abolished* is a favorite term of the apostle Paul. In 1 Corinthians he spoke of death as being the last of man's enemies to be abolished (15:56). But our Savior is not just a destroyer; he is also an illuminator who "has brought life and immortality to light" (v. 10). Life and immortality had been obscured until the coming of the Savior, but they have now been flooded with light, revealing the "mystery" of God's love for all in Christ (Eph. 3:9).

The abundant life we receive in Christ is immortal in nature. Although we still face physical death, it no longer holds us in its dread. As Paul declared in 1 Corinthians 15, the sting of death has been removed. The word "gospel" speaks of the entire revelation of God in Christ—his life, teaching, death, and resurrection.

Can you call him Savior? Have you stepped into the light of Christ and appropriated his everlasting life? Then notice how immediately Paul spoke of his desire to declare this good news (v. 11). How long has it been since you told anyone about your Savior?

# HE IS
## the Son of God

> Matthew 16:16 Simon Peter
> answered, "You are the
> Messiah, the Son of the
> living God!"

Speculation had been growing as to
the true identity of Jesus. The suggestions
ran from John the Baptist to Elijah to
Jeremiah. Yes, people were confident that
Jesus was unlike any teacher they had ever
heard, causing them to think of him as a
prophet. But all their estimations fell
profoundly short. He was not a spokesman
from God; he was God speaking in the
flesh.

In response to Jesus' query about this
to his disciples, Peter spoke for the Twelve,
declaring him to be "the Messiah, the Son
of the living God." The title "Son of God"
had likely come into use as a messianic title
in pre-Christian Judaism, indicative of
God's vice-regent in his kingdom. In later
Christian thought it was applied to Jesus
to affirm both his divine origin and nature.

First John 3:8 is another text that clari-
fies the work of the Son of God. "The one

who commits sin is of the Devil, for the Devil has sinned from the beginning. The Son of God was revealed for this purpose: to destroy the Devil's works."

The devil has been sinning from the beginning of time. This reference to "beginning" probably refers to the time when Satan first sinned against God. To suggest that sin existed before Satan's rebellion would clearly stand against the teaching of Scripture. But prior to the creation of man, the devil was already sinning. And ever since the creation of man, he has been attempting to make sin a ceaseless way of life for his followers.

Yet as John declared, "The Son of God was revealed for this purpose: to destroy the Devil's works." So when we recall that Jesus is the Son of God, we need to let this assure us that Satan is a defeated foe. Jesus has the power to undo the penalty and power of sin in your life and to loose you from its power. When you find yourself tempted to sin and you think you are too weak to resist, call upon the one who has already won the victory—Jesus Christ, The Son of God.

# HE IS
## the Son of Man

> **Matthew 9:6** The Son of Man has authority on earth to forgive sins.

What do we need most? While some might sing, "Love, sweet love," the truth is, we need forgiveness. All of mankind shares the same dilemma. We are sinners by nature and we have sinned in practice. Religion is man's attempt to discover the answer to this sin problem. But the thing religion cannot provide, the Son of Man has authority to give—forgiveness.

The title "Son of Man" occurs around eighty-four times in the Gospels, and all but one comes from the lips of Jesus. The largest number of these sayings relate to the *end of time*, when Jesus will descend to the earth to gather the elect and judge the nations. One example is found in Matthew 25:31: "When the Son of Man comes in His glory, and all the angels with Him, then He will sit on the throne of His glory."

The second largest group is connected with his *suffering*, *death*, *resurrection*, and *return*. On three occasions he predicted that the Son of Man would be rejected by men, resulting in his death and resurrection (Mk. 8:31, 9:31 and 10:33–34). The linking of the Son of Man as both Messianic Judge and Suffering Servant is unique to the teaching of Jesus. "Then the sign of the Son of Man will appear in the sky, and then all the peoples of the earth will mourn; and they will see the Son of Man coming on the clouds of heaven with power and great glory" (Mt. 24:30).

The final group of Son of Man sayings relate to *Jesus' earthly ministry*. As we have seen in the Matthew 9:6 passage, he has the authority as the Son of Man to forgive sins. In his preaching he sowed the seed of God's kingdom (Mt. 13:37), reinterpreted the Sabbath and the law (Mt. 12:8), and brought salvation to the lost (Lk. 19:10).

Aren't you glad that the Son of Man has forgiven your sin and promised you forever? He will one day gather his forgiven elect "from the four winds" (Mt. 24:31) so that we mere men might live forever with him, the Son of Man.

# HE IS
## the True Light

> John 1:9 The true light, who
> gives light to everyone, was
> coming into the world.

Reflected or partial light can play tricks on the eyes, but "true light" makes everything clear. Even familiar objects that wouldn't warrant a second glance in broad daylight can be made to look frightening or suspicious in the dark of night or in the half-lit shadows before sunrise.

Our title today occurs in the wonderful prologue to John's Gospel. John had already referred to Jesus as the pre-existent *logos* or Word of God. He then declared: "Life was in Him, and that life was the light of men" (1:4). This light penetrated the darkness and was so intense that the darkness could not overcome it. He then spoke of John the Baptist, the witness who testified about the light. John, however, was not the source of light; he could only point people to the "true light."

The word "true" captures the ideas of completeness, authenticity, dependability, and steadfastness. While some other lights may have had elements of the truth or, like John, had testified of the truth, only Jesus was the full embodiment of the truth. He did not simply bear witness to the truth; he was truth in flesh. There was and is nothing shadowy or unseen in the light Christ brings.

His light is available to all men. God has revealed something of himself to all mankind (Rom. 1:20), sufficient enough to allow them to choose the light. Yet this does not suggest that everyone will come to the light. The tragedy is found in John 1:10–11. The world he created "did not recognize Him" and "His own people did not receive Him." John repeated this tragic situation in 3:19: "This, then, is the judgment: the light has come into the world, and people loved darkness rather than the light because their deeds were evil."

Once we have "seen the light" by seeing Christ, we must bear witness to him, so that all may see and know him. Kingdom focused people are concerned that all the nations have equal opportunity to see the "true light."

# HE IS
## the True Vine

> **John 15:1** I am the true
> vine, and My Father is the
> vineyard keeper.

I inherited a great deal from my dad,
but a green thumb was not one of them.
My dad seemed to have a way with plants.
He loved roses and cultivated a love for
them in my life, although I admit I find it
easier to enjoy them than grow them.

When I planted my first roses, Dad
taught me to watch for "sucker growth,"
where the wild vine would re-emerge and
take valuable energy from the plant. He
taught me that pruning was essential if the
rose bush was to provide abundant blos-
soms.

Jesus referred to himself as the "true
vine." In the Old Testament the *vine* is
frequently used as a symbol for Israel.
Tragically, however, Israel is often pictured
as a faithless and fruitless vine, which
through disobedience had become a wild
vine (Jer. 2:21). In contrast to fruitless
Israel, however, Jesus is the "true vine,"

accomplishing perfectly that which God purposed for him.

We might expect Jesus to say that the *church* is the vine, drawing a parallelism with the wild vine of Israel. But no, Jesus is the vine. He stands as a sort of bridge or source of life between the vineyard keeper (the Father) and the branches (his church). Because he gives life to the branches, the fruit they bear is the natural consequence of abiding in him. Just as a branch is not a self-sufficient entity, neither is the believer.

The role of the Father is also decisive in this process. He watches over the vine to ensure fruitfulness. Left to itself the vine will produce unproductive growth; therefore, pruning is essential. This does not suggest that a genuine believer can be cut from the vine, but it does mean that fruitfulness is the test of belonging to the "true vine." And we can trust the vinedresser to know the difference, removing unproductive branches and cleansing productive ones so that they will be even more fruitful.

And because you are his, you will most definitely bear fruit for him, for his power flows to you from the Vine—the *True* Vine.

# HE IS
## the Truth

> **John 14:6** I am the way, the truth, and the life. No one comes to the Father except through Me.

I recall standing on the bridge of a destroyer headed from Norfolk to Yorktown, Virginia, on a short cruise. My friend, the captain of the ship, was all smiles until the ship was underway. Then I watched in fascination as he constantly monitored the ship's course.

I knew he had taken this ship out of port hundreds of times. But when I questioned him about why he was so diligent to track the course of the ship, he told me that the turbulence of the water, as well as the small opening that was provided over the bay bridge tunnel, left him no room for deviation. Truth was definitely not relative in his case.

Neither is it when it determines where we will spend eternity. Jesus had just told his disciples that he was returning to his Father. Thomas, perplexed by this announcement, asked the question everyone else must have been thinking—"We don't know where You're going. How can we know the way?" (v. 5). In response Jesus declared that he is the way, the truth, and the life. This trilogy fits naturally with each other, knitting together several themes of John's Gospel. It serves as a summation of Jesus' mission to the world.

The question of "the way" obviously raises the question of truth. If various individuals or religious groups espouse a "way" of life, how are we to know the truth of the various claims? Everyone suggests they are telling you the truth. The radical difference, though, is that Jesus does not merely *declare* the truth; he *is* the truth! Truth reminds us of the complete integrity and reliability of all that Jesus does and is.

Thus the declaration that Jesus is "the truth" does not simply speak of illumination but of revelation. Jesus is God's final word to man. God added the exclamation mark to Jesus' affirmation that He is "the truth" by establishing him "as the powerful Son of God by the resurrection from the dead according to the Spirit of holiness" (Rom. 1:4). Any questions?

# HE IS
## Wonderful

> **Isaiah 9:6** He will be named Wonderful Counselor, Mighty God, Eternal Father, Prince of Peace.

This is our fourth and final visit to Isaiah 9:6. As we read the titles applied to the child born for us, it becomes apparent they could not refer to King Ahaz's baby or any subsequent earthly child. This prophecy would not be fulfilled, in fact, for over 700 years, when a messenger of the Lord would appear to ordinary shepherds with a startling word: "Don't be afraid, for look, I proclaim to you good news of great joy that will be for all the people: today a Savior, who is Messiah the Lord, was born for you in the city of David" (Luke 2:10–11).

The context in Isaiah 9 declared that those in darkness would see a "great light" (v. 2), that their burdensome yoke would be shattered and their joy restored. When Jesus began his ministry in Capernaum, Matthew reiterated this hope. The idea of "great light" flooding the land was a favorite symbol of deliverance and of its accompanying joy and happiness. Jesus is indeed the one to bring about this "wonderful" event!

"Wonderful" indicates that Jesus exceeds the limits of human understanding and transcends the boundaries of human existence and power. When God sent an angelic messenger to Manoah to tell him of the impending birth of his son, Samson, Manoah wanted to know this angelic one's name so he could honor him. The messenger responded, "Why do you ask My name . . . since it is wonderful" (Judg. 13:18).

If the name of a messenger is wonderful, how much more the name of the Son?

Jesus once told his listeners a parable about an owner of a vineyard whose tenants killed both his messengers and his son. He then concluded the story with a quotation from Psalm 118—"The stone that the builders rejected has become the cornerstone. This came from the Lord and is wonderful in our eyes" (Matt. 21:42).

When we come to know him as Savior, this experience will fill every fiber of our being and every event of our daily existence with wonder—for he is Wonderful.

# HE IS
## the Word of God

It would be insufficient to discuss the name "Word of God" without full attention to the imagery of our Savior's dress. What is the meaning of the robe stained with blood?

Various interpreters have suggested that the blood is: (a) that of the martyrs, (b) the blood of the cross, or (c) the blood of the enemy. The latter two are the most likely. Those who suggest that the blood on the robe is the blood of the defeated enemy take their cue from the victorious conqueror pictured in Isaiah 63:1 — "Who is this coming from Edom in crimson-stained garments from Bozrah — this One who is splendid in His apparel, rising up proudly in His great might?"

Nevertheless, it is difficult not to think of the blood on his robe as the blood of Calvary. The concept of the Lamb that was slain is so integral to the book of Revelation, it is hard to dismiss it from this context. It is not impossible to think, in fact, that both ideas are present at the same time in this powerful symbol.

Christ has set us free by his blood. It is through his death that ultimate victory has been won, and thus the Lamb seen in Revelation receives glory and honor and praise. The Redeemer as well as the Judge of all the earth are one and the same — The Word of God.

This reference to "the Word" also reminds us of John's earlier writings: "In the beginning was the Word, and the Word was with God, and the Word was God" (John 1:1 and cf. 1 John 1:1). Jesus was no mere prophet speaking on behalf of God. He was God in flesh, embodying the word in his life of redemption and his judgment at the end of time. Jesus as the "Word of God" is God's final and complete word to man.

The writer of Hebrews put it this way: "Long ago God spoke to the fathers by the prophets at different times and in different ways. In these last days, He has spoken to us by His Son" (Heb. 1:1-2). He is the Word.

# HE IS
## the Way

Have you ever been lost? I mean
sufficiently lost that you swallowed your
pride and actually asked for directions?
Before the advent of GPS guidance sys-
tems, this was an all too common experience for me. I am directionally challenged.
When I am in a strange place and ask
directions, I don't want several suggestions
about optional routes. All that does is add
to my present confusion.

But confusion about earthly directions
is merely an issue of inconvenience. Confusion about *heavenly* directions has eternal
consequences.

In response to Thomas' impassioned
cry that the disciples could never join
Jesus when he returned to the Father,
Jesus declared that he is "the way." If you
read this entire section, you will notice that
"way" is repeated in verses 4, 5, and 6.
Jesus is not simply offering to guide men

to God by *revealing* the way; he is offering to bring them to God by redeeming them.

Fallen man doesn't simply need a guide to show him the way to the Father. He needs a Redeemer who can make it possible for him to enter the presence of holy God. We don't need illumination or direction; we need redemption.

That's because the way to the Father has been blocked by our sin. For us to live in the presence of holy God, we must have the way prepared by the forgiveness of our sins. And only Christ is the Way, because he alone is both God and man. "Now everything is from God, who reconciled us to Himself through Christ" (2 Cor. 5:18).

Make special note, though, that Jesus is not merely *a* way but *the* way. There is no possibility of confusion, because there are not any alternative means of approaching the Father. Only the Son of God is qualified to be "the way." So to declare that Christ is the Way is not simply praying for direction. It is the sinner's cry for provision. Have you discovered Christ as the way to the Father? If not, why not ask him to provide access to the Father for you?

# HE IS
## the Omega

> **Revelation 21:6** It is done!
> I am the Alpha and the Omega,
> the Beginning and the End.

We have a saying that someone "saves the best for last." We seem to use this most often in relation to food—in particular, dessert. We want to savor that last morsel since it is the final flavor on our tongues.

All of the great "He Is" promises are so flavorful, it would be challenging to suggest that any one of them is best. But the affirmation that "He Is Omega" is last, not only in terms of this study but because *omega* is the last letter in the Greek alphabet.

The affirmation "first and last" occurs on four occasions in the book of Revelation. At first the reference is to God, who is declared to be the beginning and end of all things—the sovereign, eternal, and transcendent one who is in control of history. What a word of encouragement this must have been to those first-century Christians who were facing persecution and death.

And even today, in spite of the chaotic appearance of the world, the promises of God can be spoken of as if already accomplished, because God's purposes in redemption are that certain. The one who created everything will oversee the new creation in the eternal order.

In chapters 21 and 22, the identical expression is applied to Christ himself, setting him apart from all created things. His authority rests in a singular fact: he shares the eternal nature of God. Thus he is the beginning and end of all history, and the Lord of all that comes between.

The translation of the phrase "It is done" is actually plural, so it can be rightly translated "*They* are done." And when all the world events that must take place have been completed, the triune God will clearly be seen as the One in command. In the end, God works all things according to his will.

He is the end of suffering, pain, and darkness—of death and of the curse! When Christ is the beginning of life for you—your Alpha—he is the culmination of all you have desired—your Omega!

# Appendix

The promises of this book are based on one's relationship to Christ. If you have not yet entered a personal relationship with Jesus Christ, I encourage you to make this wonderful discovery today. I like to use the very simple acrostic—LIFE—to explain this, knowing that God wants you not only to inherit *eternal* life but also to experience *earthly* life to its fullest.

## L = LOVE
It all begins with God's love. God created you in his image. This means you were created to live in relationship with him. *"For God loved the world in this way: He gave His One and Only Son, so that everyone who believes in Him will not perish but have eternal life" (John 3:16)*

But if God loves you and desires relationship with you, why do you feel so isolated from him?

## I = ISOLATION
This isolation is created by our sin—our rebellion against God—which separates us from him and from others. *"For all have sinned and fall short of the glory of God"* (Rom. 3:23). *"For the wages of sin is death, but the gift of God is eternal life in Christ Jesus our Lord"* (Rom. 6:23).

You might wonder how you can overcome this isolation and have an intimate relationship with God.

## F = FORGIVENESS

The only solution to man's isolation and separation from a holy God is forgiveness. *"For Christ also suffered for sins once for all, the righteous for the unrighteous, that He might bring you to God, after being put to death in the fleshly realm but made alive in the spiritual realm"* (1 Peter 3:18).

The only way our relationship can be restored with God is through the forgiveness of our sins. Jesus Christ died on the cross for this very purpose.

## E = Eternal Life

You can have full and abundant life in this present life . . . and eternal life when you die. *"But to all who did receive Him, He gave them the right to be children of God, to those who believe in His name"* (John 1:12). *"A thief comes only to steal and to kill and to destroy. I have come that they may have life and have it in abundance"* (John 10:10).

Is there any reason you wouldn't like to have a personal relationship with God?

## The Plan of Salvation

It's as simple as ABC. All you have to do is:

A = Admit you are a sinner. Turn from your sin and turn to God. *"Repent and turn back, that your sins may be wiped out so that seasons of refreshing may come from the presence of the Lord"* (Acts 3:19).

B = Believe that Jesus died for your sins and rose from the dead enabling you to have life. *"I have written these things to you who believe in the name of the Son of God, so that you may know that you have eternal life"* (1 John 5:13).

C = Confess verbally and publicly your belief in Jesus Christ. *"If you confess with your mouth, 'Jesus is Lord,' and believe in your heart that God raised Him from the dead, you will be saved. With the heart one believes, resulting in righteousness, and with the mouth one confesses, resulting in salvation"* (Rom. 10:9–10).

You can invite Jesus Christ to come into your life right now. Pray something like this:

"God, I admit that I am a sinner. I believe that you sent Jesus, who died on the cross and rose from the dead, paying the penalty for my sins. I am asking that you forgive me of my sin, and I receive your gift of eternal life. It is in Jesus' name that I ask for this gift. Amen."

Signed _____

Date _____

If you have a friend or family member who is a Christian, tell them about your decision. Then find a church that teaches the Bible, and let them help you go deeper with Christ.

## KINGDOM PROMISES

If you've enjoyed this book of Kingdom Promises, you may want to consider reading one of the others in the series:

 We Are
0-8054-2781-3

 We Can
0-8054-2780-5

 But God
0-8054-2782-1

 He Is
0-8054-2783-X

Available in stores nationwide and through major online retailers. For a complete look at Ken Hemphill titles, make sure to visit broadmanholman.com/hemphill.